Screenwriters

Screenwriters

AMERICA'S STORYTELLERS IN PORTRAIT

By Helena Lumme and Mika Manninen

ANGEL CITY PRESS

Design by Ilkka Kärkkäinen • Typographer Jere Saulivaara

Preface

A WORLD ON A PIECE OF PAPER

The composer hears a melody from within and writes it down as notes on the paper. The architect perceives a finished building as it would appear at different times of the day or year, sees people moving inside and outside, and foresees how the building will alter its surroundings.

In much the same way, the screenwriter creates on paper a world as complex and complete as the real one in which he lives.

The screenwriter visualizes his film before anyone even imagines seeing it on the screen. He creates and breathes life into characters, makes them as fallible, fascinating and incomprehensible as we all are. He laughs and cries with the characters and creates their good fortune and misfortune.

Ten minutes after the lights have dimmed in the movie theater, we are enthralled by the people on the screen, living their lives. We fall in love with the ones they love, despise those who try to get in their way (we would even kill for them if necessary!). We share their foibles, their disappointments and their moments of victory as if they were our own.

This cleverly created illusion exists from the moment the screenwriter has finished the first draft of his work.

Even though screenwriters work the same way as composers and architects, there is one essential difference: screenwriters surrender their creation to someone else. By the time the story reaches the screen, it becomes "A Film by..." the director.

When exactly does this mystical transition take place? The moment when the story is "beamed" from the brain of the screenwriter to the director, who thus becomes the *auteur*?

Directors and actors (and others) make suggestions to change the script, but that doesn't make the script theirs. To quote screenwriter Ring Lardner, Jr., "The most brilliant director in the world cannot make a good movie from a bad script — except by rewriting it and thus sharing in the screenplay credit."

SCREENWRITER, THE DISPOSABLE CREATOR

Every movie, from a small personal film to the grand sweeping epic, begins the same way. A writer gets an idea.

The writer sits down to work. For months, maybe years. The storyline has to be logical, believable, compelling. The characters have to be alive. The structure has to hold — no wasted words or scenes. And, naturally, it has to be cinematic.

When all goes well, the writer sells the script. The script attracts a cast and a director, and a movie gets made.

After that, the writer is often avoided like a disease. In many cases, he or she is not welcome or even acknowledged on the set, or at the screening, or the premiere.

If the writer happens to pick up a newspaper or magazine, or turn on a talk show, there will be the director or the actors, all talking about the wonderful film they created.

Critics write about actors and directors. Scholars look for patterns in their work. Journalists fight for interviews with them.

And collectively, curiously, everyone forgets this one basic enduring unalterable fact: a writer created the story. Everything else in the movie is built to serve that story.

Whether disregarding the screenwriter is the result of convenience or conspiracy, no one seems to know. Maybe a bit of both. Screenwriters are reluctant when it comes to fighting for their own glory. Creating movies is their first priority, securing their place in the sun is secondary.

The portraits of American screenwriters were first shown at the Cannes 50th Film Festival, at the beautiful Château de la Napoule, the center of many Cannes premiere parties.

HOLLYWOOD LEGENDS AND A BRAVE NEW GENERATION

How did we choose the subjects for this collection? Subjectively and selfishly: with our heart. We wanted to include everyone whose work has moved us.

The deeper the screenwriter penetrates our emotional world, the more universal his work becomes, touching people from Montreal to Manila. If there was life in outer space, we are sure that from there, too, we would hear the sound of sobbing as the bells tinkle over the closing frames of *It's a Wonderful Life*.

We are privileged to honor writers who made Hollywood excel: Billy Wilder, Julius Epstein, Ernest Lehman, Daniel Taradash... Apart from creating immortal films, they established a tradition and a standard by which future generations of writers could hone their skills.

We want especially to remember the blacklisted writers whose fate was to lose their names and careers to the anti-Communist persecution of the McCarthy era, when bigotry reached a level of absurdity; incomprehensible then, and even more so today.

Ring Lardner, Jr., one of the Hollywood Ten, maintained his trust in the justice offered by the Constitution of the United States. He refused to answer the questions of the House Un-American Activities Committee and was sent to prison for ten months. Twenty-eight years elapsed between his two Academy Awards. For more than half of that time Lardner and those close to him suffered under the shadow of the blacklist. Lardner continued to write scripts under a pseudonym or a front, and managed, despite fierce political discrimination, to make his debut as a novelist.

Paul Jarrico continued to write as well, and produced an independent movie, *Salt of the Earth*, in 1953. This portrayal of the working class that was made mainly by blacklisted filmmakers has become a cult movie. Thanks to Paul Jarrico's persistent work in the past decade, the Writers Guild of America has been able to restore the rightful credits of many films made during the blacklisted era.

The collection previewed at the Santa Monica Museum of Art in 1997.

Today's Hollywood has changed dramatically from the one where Wilder and Epstein arrived in the 1930s, or from the town screenwriter Fay Kanin knew two decades later. "We made films because we loved filmmaking," Kanin sighs, recalling the lost joy of the 1950s, when the words *business and industry* were not tied into film as automatically as they are today.

Despite the allegations that Hollywood has become an agents' and lawyers' medium, it might be too early to announce its death. "Hollywood is a sinking ship — and yet, from time to time someone succeeds in reaching the surface, swimming ashore and making a picture that has some meaning," notes Frank Darabont, who in his directorial debut *The Shawshank Redemption*, a film made from his screenplay, successfully made it to dry land.

Writers in this collection are individuals doing everything possible to reach the shore. They have the passion, skills and the ability to push their ideas through as survivors on the Hollywood assembly line. Instead of being in bloody combat, they offer support and a safety net to one another because they share a common goal: to make good, meaningful films.

This book is a tribute to screenwriters, the true architects of the American cinema. Thanks to their storytelling skills we fell in love with the movies and expect to fall in love each time we stand in the box-office line. Thanks to their wonderful stories directors became important directors, actors became big stars, and producers became millionaires. Thanks to their commitment to their craft, the American film industry has become a monumental business which in Los Angeles alone provides work for more than 200,000 people.

This book is a small reminder that, although a film lives before our eyes as colors and shapes on a screen, in the beginning was the word. It is all there, in the script.

HELENA LUMME

The collection's American premiere at the Academy of Motion Picture Arts and Sciences in October 1997: From left to right, William Kelley, the authors Helena Lumme and Mika Manninen, Jane Anderson, Callie Khouri, Naomi Foner, Patrick Sheane Duncan, Fay Kanin and Frank Pierson.

Fade in

When

Hitch hired me for *Marnie*, I had never even read a screenplay. My approach to narrative was totally linear, so when it came to getting Sean and Tippi from the altar to the reception to the honeymoon cabin on the ocean liner, I wrote three plodding scenes.

Hitch gently suggested that we might pick up the pace by doing this all in one scene, i.e.:

```
CLOSEUP

A large vase of roses with attached card saying
             "Congratulations."

In the vase the water sloshing, sloshing, sloshing.
```

JAY PRESSON ALLEN

Screenplays, written or co-written:

• *Deathtrap* (1982)

• *Prince of the City* (1981)

• *Just Tell Me What You Want* (1980)

• *Funny Lady* (1975)

• *Cabaret* (1972)

• *Travels With My Aunt* (1972)

• *The Prime of Miss Jean Brodie* (1969)

• *Marnie* (1964)

Film is the most collaborative

of all the arts. So if you don't want your words messed with, forget screenplays —
write a novel. When you write a film script you must be prepared to be bounced from
the loop as soon as you turn in your final draft. And if you're the practical type and
you can view your script as simply a blueprint for blockbusters that get shown in
malls, then you can cash your check and walk away. But if you're like me and tend to
write a script by hooking your vital organs directly into your computer, then the sepa-
ration can be an agony.

      Imagine giving birth to a baby, and feeding that child and changing his diapers
and staying up all night when he has the croup, and teaching him that he can't touch
the stove or hit the cat or put batteries in his mouth. And just when your kid has
become a really fun and loving and halfway-civilized human being, a bunch of people
walk into your house and say, "OK, we're going to raise him now." And they take your
kid away, change his name, give him a buzz cut and send him to military school. And
never mind your broken heart, you just hope he doesn't do any damage to society.

      I could just stick to writing plays. I could, but I don't. Because when a film col-
laboration works, when my fellow artists — the director, the actors, the cinematogra-
pher, the designers, the editor, the composer — share a passion for the story I want to
tell, then I bless whatever changes they need to make to turn my words into film. And,
I'll admit, there's nothing more thrilling than to sit there in the dark with the popcorn
crowd, watching a giant screen, and to see what I've written take on such a grand and
miraculous form.

JANE ANDERSON

Screenplays:

• *How To Make An American Quilt (1995)*

• *It Could Happen To You (1994)*

Television:

• *The Baby Dance (1998)*

• *The Positively True Adventures of the Alleged Texas
Cheerleader-Murdering Mom (1993)*

Stage plays:

• *The Baby Dance*

• *Defying Gravity*

• *Looking for Normal*

• *Lynnette at 3 a.m.*

I remember

seeing this exhibit for the first time. It was in a gallery in Santa Monica and the opening was tied in with a Writers Guild event. I remember walking into the room, and not just seeing portraits — but the writers themselves — as many as could make it. And I will never forget the feeling in there. Suffice it to say, we don't tend to gather in clumps that much. We work alone and no one really understands what we do except us. (I know — no one understands what cops or nurses do either, but at least you can see it. Try watching one of us at work sometime.)

A friend who was with me said, "All of you seem so *gentle*." And it was true.

I walked around the gallery, looking deeply at everyone's portrait while carefully dodging my own. And then I looked around at the writers themselves. And very soon, it hit me:

These were the people that taught me how to live my life.

More than my teachers, more than my rabbi and often even more than my parents — these were the bold and complicated individuals who created my heroes for me. Heroes that taught me, through their behavior, how I might behave in a tense situation. Or a loving one, or a farcical one — and I can tell you without going into it that in the most deeply critical gut-check moment of my life, when life or death actually did depend on the next action I took — it was only when I asked myself what the *hero of a movie* would do at this point, that I knew what to do. And when I got my answer, I did it. And, son of a gun — thanks to many of the writers in this collection — I got a happy ending.

Later that evening the most amazing thing happened. One of the guests came up to me, with her husband. She said she damn near almost married the wrong guy but then she saw *Sleepless in Seattle* and it gave her the courage to leave him, which led her to the right guy, whom she did marry, and now they have a kid together that they wouldn't have had if they hadn't seen that movie. My movie.

A real live kid. Another happy ending. Hollywood.

JEFF ARCH

Screenplays, written or co-written:

• *Iron Will* (1994)

• *Sleepless in Seattle* (1993)

Every

morning I visit with my family, go for a long run, and then sit down with a big cup of
coffee to start my day's work. I like to work a normal day — from ten to five or ten to
six — although more often than not that spills into evenings, weekends, or early morn-
ings. Generally I tinker with the work that's gone before as a way to recover the mood.
Then I move on to the new scene. It's a job of small victories. A day where you throw
out everything you've written but learn something about your story would have to be
considered a good day. A day where you stare into space and close up shop feeling
utterly lost and worthless would have to be considered average.

I envy writers who go to work armed with color-coded notecards, bulletin
boards, outlines, computer programs and the *scientia* of screenwriting classes. The
truth is I don't really know what I'm doing. I feel my way through it. For me so much
of it comes through my ear. The rest works itself out through the discipline of rewriting. To my mind these writers who believe their first draft is ready to shoot ought to be
dragged out behind the Guild building and horsewhipped. Rewriting is everything.

The anonymity of it is something I like. I got a good table at my favorite
restaurant for three years before they found out what I do for a living. Unconditional
love is one thing, but unconditional love from a maître d' is really something special.

PAUL ATTANASIO

Screenplays:

• *Donnie Brasco (1997)*

• *Disclosure (1994)*

• *Quiz Show (1994)*

Television:

• *Homicide: Life on the Street [creator] (1993)*

Cut to

ROBERT BENTON

Screenplays, written or co-written:

• Twilight (1998)

• Nobody's Fool (1994)

• Billy Bathgate (1991)

• Nadine (1987)

• Places in the Heart (1984) *AA*

• Still of the Night (1982)

• Kramer vs. Kramer (1979) *AA*

• The Late Show (1977)

• Bad Company (1972)

• What's Up, Doc? (1972)

• There Was a Crooked Man (1970)

• Bonnie and Clyde (1967)

The first time

we met, Mika said, "I'd like to do something '40s."

Music to my ears. Though as a writer I'm hardly known for toiling in the noble vineyards of hard-boiled noir, I do count among my literary gods the estimable Raymond Chandler. I also yearn in a most embarrassing fashion for a Los Angeles that no longer exists — indeed, may never have existed outside the romantic realm of Mr. Chandler's fiction. For me, the thought of getting duded up in Philip Marlowe drag was irresistible.

Los Angeles is a metropolis ever in flux, yet old landmarks peer from her nooks and crannies like welcome ghosts of a bygone age. One such revenant is the Body-snatcher Bridge — so nicknamed because Kevin McCarthy once ran pell-mell across it in the middle of a movie traffic jam, pounding on windshields and shouting hysterical warnings to anybody who might listen: the pod people are coming, they're real, they're here, *you're next!* Most folks driving the Hollywood Freeway through the Cahuenga Pass zip under this lovely old bridge blissfully unaware of its significance, but perhaps you'll spare it a kind thought next time you motor by doing seventy-five in the fast lane. For our purposes, it seemed a likely place to indulge in a little retro-noir.

I showed up packing heat and a teddy bear. Mika did a swell double-take and asked the inevitable: "Why a teddy bear?"

"Get wise, shutterbug," I snarled. "The bad guys of this world just pack heat. The good guys pack teddy bears as well, metaphorically speaking. It has to do with keeping a childlike heart, for without a childlike heart one cannot seek truth and justice, and will surely be swallowed by darkness and corruption."

Or words to that effect. I forget exactly. Mika just shrugged and told me he thought the teddy bear was really weird and cool, so we went with it.

I like to think that writers and fictional detectives share a spiritual kinship. We work alone, plumbing the back alleys and mean streets of the soul in search of some higher meaning or truth. We get bloodied from time to time in the quest, but every so often a glimmer of truth does prevail . . . and, believe me, that's enough to keep you walking those mean streets for a long, long time.

Just come packing heat, and don't forget your teddy bear.

FRANK DARABONT

Screenplays:

• *The Green Mile (1999)*

• *The Shawshank Redemption (1994)*

Television:

• *The Young Indiana Jones Chronicles*
  [seven episodes] (1992-93)

Let's talk

about the most important talent every writer needs to succeed in the film business. Perseverance.

Perseverance. It's more important than talent.

Perseverance. Right now you're beating your head against a big wall — huge, granite stones. The stones have names. "Development Executives." "No relatives in the business." "You went to the wrong prep school." "Development Executives." "Nobody can read." "Not a member of the Writers Guild." "NBC, Paramount, Universal, Warner Brothers, ABC, Showtime, Fox (studio and network)." "Development . . ."

A lot of rocks. A big wall.

And every day you sit in front of a blank piece of paper, a computer screen, a typewriter, for the nostalgic few, or a tablet, for us Cro-Magnon types, and beat your head against that wall.

Got a headache?

Get used to it. Believe me, there is a whole gauntlet of walls behind this one.

But let's deal with this first big wall. And the biggest rocks in that wall. Rejection — Mediocrity — Self-Defeat.

REJECTION

At first it seems impossible to get someone to read your scripts. You're writing in a vacuum. You keep getting them mailed back to you — unread. You think you might as well mail the damn thing straight to yourself, eliminate the middleman and cut the postage in half.

Even if you get them to read your script, they never call you and if you get any response at all, it's that nasty, curt little form letter. "Sorry, but our needs right now . . . keep trying." And God forbid you finally get that meeting and they sit there, eyes glazed over from too much wine at Le Dôme and glance at their watches every fifteen seconds because they don't want to miss Jerry Springer (story ideas). They call the guy who details their Porsche, then shake your hand, get your name wrong and as they walk you to the door, ask if you've heard of any openings at Joel Silver's company.

Rejection.

Every time you get rejected, do what I do. I tear up that letter, I walk out of the meeting, I glare at the phone and say to myself, "What the hell do they know, the ignorant, arrogant, illiterate, over-paid, ass-kissing, pandering pederasts? One of these days they'll be kissing *my* ass." Of course the next question is why you would want some ignorant, arrogant, illiterate, over-paid, pandering pederast to put his or her lips to your butt. Don't ask that question — ever.

Rejection. Deal with it. Accept it as a fact of life, like snails. Go ahead and step on them, but don't slip and break your neck. If only you could pour salt on the slimy bastards and watch them fizz and curl up and die . . . Sorry.

Rejection. Deal with it.

MEDIOCRITY

I know you see a lot of bad movies and bad TV and wonder what the hell you are doing working so hard trying to write great scripts when all this crap is getting made. There you are, working on your plot when ninety percent of the things you watch don't make any more sense than Louis Farrakhan's speech at the Mall. Why work so hard trying to give characters life and then witness Sly Stallone sleepwalk his way through films like another Ken doll on steroids — and see it make a hundred jillion dollars? Why should you painstakingly try to write clever, articulate dialogue only to hear the phrase, "Oh, fuck," and its witty counterpart, "Oh, shit," repeated between gunshots and be nominated for an Oscar for Best Screenplay?

But just because these films are successful is no justification for you to slack off. To write badly or to write down to an audience is the worst sin. And remember, quite a few of these films started out as decent scripts. It's hard to see how . . . but you'd be surprised at how thorough actors, producers and directors are at screwing up a good screenplay. They have years of experience so they've gotten really good at it.

The fact that mediocre scripts get made, or good scripts get made mediocre, is no justification to aim low. You can't. You have to write better than anyone else. You have to shine. Remember, these hacks already have the job. You don't. You need to stand out, make yourself unique. Do it with quality.

SELF-DEFEAT

Don't beat yourself up. There are too many people lined up to take a punch at you as it is. Times get tough.

Hey, welcome to Life 101. Just because you are in a rut in your career, don't let it become one for your writing. You will have bad days. We all do. In your worst days seek out the comfort of friends, your spouse, lover, your mother, somebody who will read your latest opus and give you an attaboy.

Write on.

Take satisfaction from the writing itself. From your friends' nice words. "Nice story." "Funny line." "I cried." "I laughed." "I pissed my pants."

Keep pounding at the wall.

It's high. It's thick. It's hard.

But take comfort from this simple fact: It is those who persevere who win. Some drop out. A few are crushed by falling rocks.

Stock up on Tylenol.

And keep ramming your head against the granite. Because if you really want to be a writer, there is obviously something very wrong with you . . . and part of that abnormality is that your skull is extremely thick.

One day that wall will go down. And as the dust and rock settle, you can see the next wall behind it.

Welcome to show business.

— *From Duncan's magazine ScreenWriter Quarterly, Fall 1996.*

PATRICK SHEANE DUNCAN

Screenplays:

• *Courage Under Fire (1996)*

• *Mr. Holland's Opus (1995)*

• *Nick of Time (1994)*

• *A Home of Our Own (1993)*

• *84 Charlie Mopic (1989)*

Screenplay by. Original Story by. Hmph! Audiences don't know somebody sits down and writes a picture. They think actors make it up as they go along.

Here is what

I always say about screenwriting. When you write a script, it's like delivering a great big beautiful plain pizza, the one with only cheese and tomatoes. And then you give it to the director, and the director says, "I love this pizza. I am willing to commit to this pizza. But I really think this pizza should have mushrooms on it." And you say, "Mushrooms! Of course! I meant to put mushrooms on the pizza! Why didn't I think of that? Let's put some on immediately." And then someone else comes along and says, "I love this pizza too, but it really needs green peppers." "Great," you say. "Green peppers. Just the thing." And then someone else says, "Anchovies." There's always a fight over the anchovies. And when you get done, what you have is a pizza with everything. Sometimes it's wonderful. And sometimes you look at it and you think, I knew we shouldn't have put the green peppers onto it. Why didn't I say so at the time? Why didn't I lie down in traffic to prevent anyone's putting green peppers onto the pizza?

— From the introduction to the Knopf edition of *When Harry Met Sally*, 1990.

NORA EPHRON

Screenplays, written or co-written:

• *You've Got Mail (1998)*

• *Michael (1996)*

• *Mixed Nuts (1994)*

• *Sleepless in Seattle (1993)*

• *This is My Life (1992)*

• *My Blue Heaven (1990)*

• *When Harry Met Sally (1989)*

• *Cookie (1989)*

• *Heartburn (1986)*

• *Silkwood (1983)*

I´ve often been

asked how the finish came about in *Casablanca*. Well, you've never witnessed such consternation in a studio. When we were about three-quarters into the picture, we ran out of story. We could not use the rest of the story of the play, because in the play, not only does Bogart not shoot Major Strassen, but Major Strassen arrests Bogart and takes him off to jail as the curtain comes down, which is a very unsatisfactory ending.

I think there were seventy-five writers on the contract, and Warner had seventy-five writers trying to think of an ending. They were stopping people on the streets asking if they had any ideas . . .

My brother and I were driving to the studio – don't forget we were twins – and just below Beverly Glen Boulevard, we turned to each other and said: "Round up the usual suspects." And in the half hour that it took to drive from Beverly Glen to the studio, we had the ending all blocked out, and it took maybe two afternoons to write it.

Now there are lot of stories that there were two endings, written and shot. Absolutely untrue. That was the ending, and it always was the ending. But the way we wrote the scene, the Bogart character did not say: "This is the beginning of a beautiful friendship." It was given to Claude Rains. And Bogart said it to him. Our last line was Bogart saying: "Yes, but don't forget you still owe me ten thousand francs."

Now we'll never know whether that line would have been better . . .

— From the Writers Guild Foundation series *The Writer Speaks*, 1995.

Julius and Philip Epstein shared an Oscar with Howard Koch for adapting the unproduced play "Everyone Comes to Rick´s" into *Casablanca*.

JULIUS EPSTEIN

Screenplays, written or co-written:

- *Reuben, Reuben* (1983)
- *House Calls* (1978)
- *Pete 'n' Tillie* (1972)
- *Fanny* (1961)
- *Take a Giant Step* (1959)
- *Tall Story* (1960)
- *The Tender Trap* (1955)
- *The Last Time I Saw Paris* (1954)
- *Romance on the High Seas* (1948)
- *Arsenic and Old Lace* (1944)
- *Mr. Skeffington* (1944)
- *Casablanca* (1943) *AA*
- *The Male Animal* (1942)
- *The Man Who Came to Dinner* (1941)
- *The Strawberry Blonde* (1941)
- *No Time for Comedy* (1940)
- *Four Wives* (1939)
- *Four Daughters* (1938)

Writing for me is like photography.

It's about observing and locating within a frame line a small story that grows on you, because it's emblematic of things we all go through. I think the writer's job is to move an audience enough to make them think. To put a face on a problem. To allow an audience to know it.

To do this, characters need to be as specific as possible. It's the details that are moving. God is in the details. When you know who your characters are, they write themselves. They can only do certain things. They can only say certain things.

Film is a powerful medium and I believe it needs to be used with special responsibility. It tells much of its story without words. What gets left out is as powerful as what is seen. For decades there were no Black faces or smart women. And where is middle age now?

My struggle as a writer is to write in images. To use the medium to its full potential. Subtext is more powerful than monologue. Again, what gets left unsaid is saying something.

I don't trust any writer who says they like to write. It hurts. It's hard to do. I love to collaborate. I miss being in a community. I learn the most when I get to go along when the movie is made. That's the fun, even though it's like watching a sweater you've knitted be unraveled. Editing is writing again. Sometimes, the sweater ends up with three arms. It's amazing how a movie is more or less than the sum of its parts. Sometimes, it's Jello, sometimes it's a bowl of red water.

My writing has always been done amidst the chaos of life. First, among diapers and baby bottles. Now in the spaces left to me between phone calls and choral concerts and screenings and meals. I hope this has all found its way into my work.

For a woman, it's always a struggle between the nurturing of motherhood and family and the selfishness of creating. Sometimes, I've chosen the children (my greatest work) and I've wanted them to thank me for it. And of course, they took it as their birthright. That's as it should be. I'm so glad for them. They teach me every day. As does my husband. Who says it should be easy?

I long for a cabin in the woods, quiet music and a sandwich of fresh bread outside my door, but I wonder if I could actually work if I didn't have the opera that is my life around me.

NAOMI FONER

Screenplays:

• *Losing Isaiah (1995)*

• *A Dangerous Woman (1993)*

• *Running on Empty (1988)*

• *Violets Are Blue (1986)*

I don't

think of myself as a screenwriter, but as a playwright who is fortunate
enough from time to time to be asked to write a screenplay. A job I take
very seriously when asked and hope the results bring some dignity to
an often much-maligned profession.

HORTON FOOTE

Screenplays:

• *Of Mice and Men (1992)*

• *On Valentine's Day (1986)*

• *The Trip to Bountiful (1985)*

• *1918 (1985)*

• *Tender Mercies (1983) AA*

• *Tomorrow (1972)*

• *Baby the Rain Must Fall (1965)*

• *To Kill a Mockingbird (1962) AA*

Stage plays:

• *Laura Dennis*

• *Night Seasons*

• *Talking Pictures*

• *The Trip to Bountiful*

• *Vernon Early*

• *The Young Men from Atlanta*

My father,

an airline pilot, once described flying as "ninety-nine percent sheer boredom and one percent sheer terror." Well, for me, writing is the exact opposite. I'm never bored when I sit down to work, but I'm always scared shitless. I have no idea what I'm doing, where I'm going, or why anyone would pay me to do it in the first place. I have yet to deliver a script to a producer and say, "Yep, I nailed it." Instead, the way it usually goes, as soon as I hand over the draft, I immediately get the flu.

However, I do find some small comfort in the fact that I'm in excellent company.

Samuel Beckett, a guy who knew from angst, said that "Suffering is the main condition of the artistic experience."

Malcom Lowry must have just spent a long night proofreading *Under the Volcano* when he said, "Fear ringed by doubt is my eternal moon."

But it was William Styron who put it best when he said, "Let's face it, writing is hell."

Amen.

I keep these and similar quotes taped to the underside of my desk. That way, when I'm lying on the floor, clutching my twisted gut, I can look up and read them and feel better.

Now, an extremely cynical person might say, *Yeah, but those guys were REAL writers, not screenwriters. And based on the few movies I've seen lately, I gotta wonder: how hard could it be?*

Cut to

Judging by the piles of unsolicited screenplays that studios receive each month, there are a lot of people out there who feel the same way. Screenwriting's easy. And you know what? It's true. Anyone with pencil and paper can write a script. The same way anyone with a brush and a tube of gouache can paint a picture.

But the pain doesn't come from just doing it. It comes from trying to do it well; from knowing in your mind's eye what *good* is, yet feeling impotent in your attempts to get it out of your head and onto the page.

The truth is that good writing is difficult to achieve no matter what the medium. Call me crazy, but I don't think it was any easier for Frank Pierson to write *Dog Day Afternoon* than it was for John Updike to write *Rabbit is Rich*. I would bet anything that both of those guys found the work agonizing.

Okay, if it's such a torture, why do it? Good question. For me the answer is simple: while I may be miserable while I'm writing, I'm a lot more miserable when I'm not.

I call it "The Golfer Syndrome."

You watch someone play golf, for seventeen holes they could be cussing and screaming and hurling their clubs into the water hazard, but on the last hole, they hit a perfect shot and . . . Bingo. All those lousy shots are suddenly forgotten and they can't wait to get back on the course again the next day.

There are moments like that when we write, when it all comes together, that are like the perfect golf shot; where all the pain and torment that came before is instantly rendered irrelevant. Instead, we sit there and read and re-read that single line of dialogue, that tiny piece of description, that odd name we came up with for the corpse, and we can't wait for tomorrow.

SCOTT FRANK

Screenplays, written or co-written:

• *Out of Sight (1998)*

• *Get Shorty (1995)*

• *Heaven's Prisoners (1996)*

• *Malice (1993)*

• *Little Man Tate (1991)*

• *Dead Again (1991)*

There must be a better way of

not making a living.

– Paul Jarrico

BO GOLDMAN

Screenplays, written or co-written

• Meet Joe Black (1998)

• City Hall (1996)

• Scent of a Woman (1992)

• Shoot The Moon (1982)

• Melvin and Howard (1980) *AA*

Don't blame the photographers.

I had eye surgery that day.

WILLIAM GOLDMAN

Screenplays:

• *Absolute Power* (1997)

• *The Ghost and the Darkness* (1996)

• *Maverick* (1994)

• *Misery* (1990)

• *The Princess Bride* (1987)

• *Magic* (1978)

• *A Bridge Too Far* (1977)

• *All the President's Men* (1976) *AA*

• *Marathon Man* (1976)

• *The Great Waldo Pepper* (1975)

• *Butch Cassidy and the Sundance Kid* (1969) *AA*

• *Harper* (1966)

Screenwriting is like having sex,

only different.

BUCK HENRY

Screenplays, written or co-written:

• To Die For (1995)

• Protocol (1984)

• First Family (1980)

• The Day of the Dolphin (1973)

• What's Up, Doc? (1972)

• The Owl and the Pussycat (1971)

• Catch 22 (1970)

• The Graduate (1967)

My Country: Right the Wrong

The Guilds have come a long way since they failed to protect the Hollywood Ten and the Hollywood hundreds. What you and your fellow presidents have reaffirmed tonight is the guiding principle of unionism: that an injury to one is an injury to all. In Budd Schulberg's novel *What Makes Sammy Run?*, Sammy has lied and cheated and knifed his way up the ladder to become head of a major studio. As he surveys his domain from the window of his penthouse, glowing with satisfaction, the writer who is telling the story asks him how he feels. Sammy considers this. "Patriotic," he says.

As we heard, Parnell Thomas said to Ring Lardner, Jr. "Any real American would be proud to answer that question. Any real American." And of course the next question: "Who else?" Patriotism defined as your willingness to betray others. Do it to show that you love your country. Refuse to do it and you're in contempt of Congress, a Congress beneath contempt. Patriotism: a contradictory word, for the history of our country is contradictory. I think of it as a double helix, two strands of history intertwined. One strand is brutal slavery, the genocide visited upon Native Americans, the ugly waves of know-nothing bigotry that have greeted every wave of immigration, women subordinated, labor strikes broken by force of arms, lynching, periodic repression of dissent. The other strand is noble history: the abolitionists, the suffragettes, the ongoing fight to end racism, to end sexism, to end the obscene chasm between poverty and wealth. Our brutal history defines patriotism as "My country right or wrong." Our noble history refines it as "My country: Right the wrong." Right the wrong. It may take another fifty years, but we shall overcome. The good guys will win.

— Paul Jarrico's words at "Hollywood Remembers the Blacklist," a fifty-year commemorative event produced by the leading guilds of Hollywood on October 27, 1997. The following day he died in a car crash.

PAUL JARRICO

Screenplays, written or co-written:
- *Messenger of Death (1988)*
- *Assassination in Sarajevo (1977)*
- *All Night Long (1961)*
- *Five Branded Women (1960)*
- *The Girl Most Likely (1957)*
- *The Paris Express (1953)*
- *The White Tower (1950)*
- *Not Wanted (1949)*
- *The Search (1943)*
- *Song of Russia (1943)*
- *Thousands Cheer (1943)*
- *Tom, Dick and Harry (1941)*

I was

writing novels and short stories for ten years before I ever wrote a screenplay. Since then I have been alternating between books and screenplays and have so far written eighteen of each. I'm not aware of taking a different approach with one or the other. Whether I'm writing films or fiction, I feel I'm always the same writer with the same concerns — about making a story move; about establishing interesting characters and developing the relationships between them. The only difference is that with the books it's all up to me, whereas with the screenplays there are many talents to make it all come alive. And since I've always worked with the same team — James Ivory and Ismail Merchant — I've been able to hand over my scripts to them, confident that they will bring out whatever is good in my work as well as counterbalancing my unabashedly literary imagination with their own, much more visual, cinematic one. They also take care of the business and other such aspects — I've never had to meet a financier! — leaving me a carefree and contented scriptwriter.

RUTH PRAWER JHABVALA

Screenplays:

• *Surviving Picasso* (1996)

• *Jefferson in Paris* (1995)

• *The Remains of the Day* (1993)

• *Howards End* (1992) *AA*

• *Mr. and Mrs. Bridge* (1990)

• *A Room With a View* (1986) *AA*

• *The Bostonians* (1984)

• *Heat and Dust* (1983)

• *Shakespeare Wallah* (1965)

Books:

• *Shards of Memory* (1995)

• *Three Continents* (1987)

• *Out of India* (1986)

• *Heat and Dust* (1975)

• *Travelers* (1971)

• *Esmond in India* (1958)

My husband,

Michael, and I collaborated on plays and screenplays for many years. I must confess that he enjoyed the actual act of writing more than I did. Since he was also an accomplished writer of verse, he decided to memorialize my attitude in the following:

Fay's Sin

Writing is something one has to admire,
The art and the craft are a constant delight.
How great for the ego to sway, to inspire,
The fly in the ointment is having to write.

Creating a manuscript, even a stinker,
Requires an effort that boggles the mind.
My God, all that sitting, like Rodin's "The Thinker,"
Can seriously damage your brain and behind.

For forty-odd years in this noble profession
I've harbored a guilt and my conscience is smitten.
So here is my rather embarrassed confession —
I don't like to write, but I love to have written.

— Michael Kanin

I dedicate this page to Michael, who I trust is now writing solo in the heavenly community.

FAY KANIN

Screenplays, written or co-written:
- *Teacher's Pet* (1958)
- *The Opposite Sex* (1956)
- *Rhapsody* (1954)

Television:
- *Heartsounds* (1984)
- *Friendly Fire* (1979)
- *Hustling* (1975)
- *Tell Me Where it Hurts* (1974)

I'm

interested in the conflict between our ideals and our desires; that's where the drama is for me. We know how we're supposed to act, but we're constantly in rebellion against the things we've been taught. Our hearts and bodies are telling us other things. That's true from *Body Heat* right through to *Mumford* — you have an idea how you should lead your life, but it's very difficult to live up to that.

LAWRENCE KASDAN

Screenplays, written or co-written:

• *Mumford* (1999)

• *Wyatt Earp* (1994)

• *The Bodyguard* (1992)

• *Grand Canyon* (1991)

• *The Accidental Tourist* (1988)

• *Silverado* (1985)

• *The Big Chill* (1983)

• *Return of the Jedi* (1983)

• *Body Heat* (1981)

• *Continental Divide* (1981)

• *Raiders of the Lost Ark* (1981)

• *The Empire Strikes Back* (1980)

Many writers feel terror facing

a blank page. To me, it's the opposite. Like the blank screen, the naked first page is often the most exhilarating sight of all, for it says that anything is possible, anything could happen here; the only limits are my talent and imagination. Then I type the first sentence and "only" becomes something devastating and immense.

NICHOLAS KAZAN

Screenplays, written or co-written:

• *Fallen (1998)*

• *Matilda (1996)*

• *Dream Lover (1994)*

• *Reversal of Fortune (1990)*

• *Patty Hearst (1988)*

• *At Close Range (1986)*

• *Frances (1982)*

Why do you write for the screen?

Why go through the agonies of visualizing every instant of film, of particularizing every aspect of every location and every scene, of anticipating and specifying every nuance of every expression and every line, of telling your story without self-indulgence or rambling or the least inattention to pace and structure, and of, finally, surrendering your carved-in-the-heart script to a producer and a director and a casting director, none of whom may know or discern what your vision was, is, or might be — attending always to their own visions of box office, auteurism, or starpower?

Why write for the screen? Because, simply and existentially, it is the most direct route to big money.

WILLIAM KELLEY

Screenplays, written or co-written:

• *Witness* (1985) *AA*

Television:

• *Gunsmoke*

• *Bonanza*

• *Kung Fu*

• *How the West Was Won*

• *The Winds of Kitty Hawk*

• *The Blue Lightning*

• *The Demon Murder Case*

Books:

• *Witness* (1985)

• *The Tyree Legend* (1979)

• *The God Hunters* (1964)

• *Gemini* (1959)

I fell into screenwriting much like Alice fell down the rabbit hole.

And now I'm in a world that makes about as much sense.

CALLIE KHOURI

Screenplays:

• *Something To Talk About* (1995)

• *Thelma and Louise* (1991) *AA*

Hollywood may yet survive … If only about a thousand suits would drink some hemlock and leave on the next rocket to Heaven´s Gate.   - William Kelley

I think

anyone who lives a creative life is somewhat an outcast. It's important, in a way. The job is to offer perspectives, insights, images that don't jibe with the collective or are out of the ordinary. But the tug of war is ever present. The need to be accepted and seen is always pulling on the necessity of remaining an outlaw to the socially accepted, if you want to leave a mark with your work. Look at the seventies; all the eye-opening breakthroughs came from fighting tough opposition, with nobody believing in it. I like that. Success and comfort can be killers to imagination. That's why I spend a good deal of time nurturing my psychotic paranoia and enormous insecurities.

Movies are our modern myths. The gods and goddesses on the screen guide us through many lifetimes. And like the ancients sitting around the fire listening to the storyteller, every now and then we see ourselves in the stories. And come away with a little understanding. Or not. Maybe for two hours or so, we are simply allowed to leave behind the life we lead and feel safe . . . feel elated . . . feel thrilled . . . see somebody else suffering instead of ourselves . . . catch our breath . . . and we're entertained. Entertainment is not a shallow gift. Sometimes, it's the only part of the day we can remember with gratitude.

RICHARD LAGRAVENESE

Screenplays, written or co-written:

- *Living Out Loud (1998)*
- *Beloved (1998)*
- *The Horse Whisperer (1998)*
- *The Mirror Has Two Faces (1996)*
- *The Bridges of Madison County (1995)*
- *Unstrung Heroes (1995)*
- *A Little Princess (1995)*
- *The Ref (1994)*
- *The Fisher King (1991)*

On Thursday, October 30, 1947,

the Chairman of the House Un-American Activities Committee, J. Parnell Thomas, questions Ring Lardner, Jr.

J. PARNELL THOMAS: Any real American would be proud to answer the question [on Communist Party membership]. Any real American.

RING LARDNER, Jr.: It depends on the circumstances. I could answer it, but if I did, I'd hate myself in the morning.

THE CHAIRMAN: Leave the witness chair!

MR. LARDNER: It is a question that would —

THE CHAIRMAN: Leave the witness chair!

MR. LARDNER: Because it is a question —

THE CHAIRMAN (pounding gavel): Leave the witness chair!

MR. LARDNER: I think I am leaving by force.

THE CHAIRMAN: Sergeant, take the witness away!

Ring Lardner, Jr., as one of the Hollywood Ten, was to spend ten months in a federal prison as a result of this exchange. He was blacklisted for fifteen years. Twenty-eight years elapsed between his two Academy Awards.

RING LARDNER, JR

Screenplays, written or co-written:
- *The Greatest* (1977)
- *M*A*S*H* (1970) *AA*
- *The Cincinnati Kid* (1965)
- *A Breath of Scandal* (1960)
- *Virgin Island* (1959)
- *The Forbidden Street* (1949)
- *Forever Amber* (1947)
- *Cloak and Dagger* (1946)
- *Brotherhood of Man* (1945)
- *Tomorrow the World* (1944)
- *The Cross of Lorraine* (1943)
- *Woman of the Year* (1942) *AA*
- *The Courageous Dr. Christian* (1940)
- *Meet Dr. Christian* (1939)

Books:
- *The Ecstasy of Owen Muir* (1955)
- *The Lardners: My Family Remembered* (1976)
- *All for Love* (1985)

"Somewhere in my youth or childhood, I must have done something good."

— From *The Sound of Music*. Music and lyrics by Richard Rodgers and Oscar Hammerstein II.

ERNEST LEHMAN

Screenplays, written or co-written:

• Black Sunday (1977)

• Family Plot (1976)

• Portnoy's Complaint (1972)

• Hello Dolly! (1969)

• Who's Afraid of Virginia Woolf? (1966)

• The Sound of Music (1965)

• West Side Story (1961)

• North By Northwest (1959)

• The Sweet Smell of Success (1957)

• The King and I (1956)

• Somebody Up There Likes Me (1956)

• Sabrina (1954)

• Executive Suite (1954)

I know most

people wouldn't agree with me, but I think the screenwriter has the best job in the movies. The screenwriter knows the first moment of desire. The impulse. That's my favorite part: the overwhelming sensation that you know how to do this one, odd, solitary task. First drafts. No one asks any questions — for a while, at least, no one has any opinions.

Then it can all go any which way. I've been terribly lucky in generally liking which way things went. But, the finished movies were not necessarily how I imagined them.

There was a moment in Morocco last fall, where Martin Scorsese was directing *Kundun*, a script I wrote, when someone nonchalantly mentioned to me the scaffolding he had erected against a distant mountain. Why scaffolding? The art department was painting a Buddha on the mountainside? Why? Because it was in the script.

I remembered the impulse to create a world where Buddha was painted on mountainsides. He was in the first draft. But, I couldn't believe that anyone had actually gone out into the desert and painted one. I never saw this Moroccan Buddha in person; I've yet to see it on film. I'm pretty sure it will not be the Buddha I imagined: not the posture or the colors or the lighting. Not the angle or the composition. But, none of those were my job. This particular Buddha passed from me to others. My job was to have the desire to imagine him.

MELISSA MATHISON

Screenplays, written or co-written:

• *Kundun* (1997)

• *The Indian in the Cupboard* (1995)

• *Twilight Zone: The Movie* (1983)

• *E.T.: the Extraterrestrial* (1982)

• *The Escape Artist* (1982)

• *The Black Stallion* (1979)

Television:

• *Son of the Morning Star* (1991)

I love

the routine of writing. The day-after-day process of sitting down and doing it. I like the empty feeling at the end of the day and the fullness at the beginning of the next. I like the jittery feeling I have when I turn on my computer and adjust myself in my chair like a pianist about to perform. But the part I like best is absolutely never knowing what the day will bring, never knowing when an idea will come that makes my heart race and my fingers fly over the keyboard. Cole Porter said, "Work is more fun than fun." How lucky I am to understand what he meant.

— Nancy Meyers

Nancy once told me

that she thought writing together was romantic. I think it's one of the nicest things anyone's ever said to me.

— Charles Shyer

NANCY MEYERS and CHARLES SHYER

Screenplays, written or co-written:

- The Parent Trap (1998)
- Father of the Bride Part II (1995)
- I Love Trouble (1994)
- Father of the Bride (1991)
- Baby Boom (1987)
- Irreconcilable Differences (1984)
- Private Benjamin (1980)

Tennyson said

a good hymn — which is a song to God — is the most difficult thing to write, because it has to be both poetry and ordinary, to span the exalted and the commonplace. Same things are true of a good screenplay.

FRANK PIERSON

Screenplays, written or co-written:

• *Presumed Innocent (1990)*

• *In Country (1989)*

• *Dog Day Afternoon (1975) AA*

• *The Anderson Tapes (1971)*

• *Cool Hand Luke (1967)*

• *Cat Ballou (1965)*

My first job in the business

was writing obituaries — twenty-five bucks a dead man, payable upon decease. Harry Truman got better so many times he nearly starved me to death. But at least I learned I prefer the living.

After that, I became a police reporter in a Navy town, covering the back-street frolics of submarine sailors on a shore leave after months under the polar ice cap. Once again, it was a great education. In this case, a sex education — especially for a convent-educated girl unaccustomed to reading police reports. I also learned a lot about characters, human foibles and the fun to be had from observing them. Not to mention indulging myself in some of the most savory foibles on a fairly regular basis.

Perhaps it was inevitable that I turn eventually to black comedy. Of course there was a fifteen-year diversion into television news, *60 Minutes* and the documentary film business. But I count that, too, as part of my education: how to say "Yes, Boss" when a person with power is tearing the heart out of something you've slaved to create, how to chip away at the innocuous elements of reality in order to get at the pithy bits, how to order ham sandwiches in forty different languages. A ham sandwich being the cleanest thing you could hope to get in a number of places I volunteered to go during The Diversion. And clean being much preferable to a two-day bout of green-apple quickstep while the film crew sits around, their hours eating very scarce money.

The education continues of course. Teaching me mostly now how little I really know. And how much I wish I did. And how easy it is to long for the days when the flesh was firm and the heart soft, instead of vice versa. And how hard it is to keep heart, eyes and spirit facing forward when gravity pulls — not so much down as back.

Perhaps that's why I teach now. Every hour in a classroom teaches me far more than I can possibly teach them. Plus, it's the only way I've yet discovered to stave off that most gruesome affliction of advancing age — incipient old-farthood.

JANET ROACH

Screenplays, written or co-written:

• *Mr. North* (1988)

• *Prizzi's Honor* (1985)

If the opening credits list only one screenwriter, chances

are the movie will be good.   - Jane Anderson

Put it on my tombstone:

"*Finally, a plot!*"

ALVIN SARGENT

Screenplays, written or co-written:

- *Anywhere But Here* (1999)
- *Other People's Money* (1991)
- *White Palace* (1990)
- *Dominick and Eugene* (1988)
- *Nuts* (1987)
- *Ordinary People* (1980) *AA*
- *Straight Time* (1978)
- *Julia* (1977) *AA*
- *Bobby Deerfield* (1977)
- *Paper Moon* (1973)
- *Love and Pain and the Whole Damn Thing* (1973)
- *The Effect of Gamma Rays on Man-in-the-Moon Marigolds* (1972)
- *I Walk the Line* (1970)
- *The Sterile Cuckoo* (1969)
- *The Stalking Moon* (1968)
- *Gambit* (1966)

I love movies.

But I love theater more. I love theater more because if a writer writes for the movies, sooner or later he's someone's lackey. Unless he also directs. What I like best about writing is losing myself in an imaginary set of circumstances. So spending time directing is not appealing to me. But I recently decided to spend more time writing for the movies. There's no action in the theater for a writer who can't hold a tune or write jokes. I'm enjoying writing movies. More so than in the past. The reason is that I recently decided that having money is more satisfying than writing a good play.

MURRAY SCHISGAL

Screenplays, written or co-written:

• *Tootsie (1982)*

• *The Tiger Makes Out (1967)*

Television:

• *Natasha Kovolina Pipshinsky (1976)*

• *The Love Song of Barney Kempinski (1966)*

Stage plays:

• *Slouching Towards the Millennium (1997)*

• *Circus Life (1995)*

• *Extensions (1994)*

• *Popkins (1990)*

• *Road Show (1987)*

• *Twice Around the Park (1982)*

• *The Pushcart Peddlers (1979)*

• *An American Millionaire (1974)*

• *All Over Town (1974)*

• *The Chinese and Dr. Fish (1970)*

• *Jimmy Shine (1968)*

• *Fragments and the Basement (1967)*

• *Luv (1963)*

• *The Typist & the Tiger (1960)*

"Everybody

wants to talk. It's like a compulsion. My philosophy is: you got nothing to say, don't say it. They figure out you can tell a drug dealer anything, things they would never tell anyone else. He understands. Of course they're stoned to start. If I could tie together all the hours of coke talk I've heard, that would be a lot of string."

— John LeTour in *Light Sleeper.*

PAUL SCHRADER

Screenplays, written or co-written:

• *Affliction* (1998)

• *Touch* (1997)

• *City Hall* (1996)

• *Light Sleeper* (1992)

• *The Last Temptation of Christ* (1988)

• *Light of Day* (1987)

• *The Mosquito Coast* (1986)

• *Mishima: A Life in Four Chapters* (1985)

• *Raging Bull* (1980)

• *American Gigolo* (1980)

• *Old Boyfriends* (1979)

• *Hardcore* (1979)

• *Blue Collar* (1978)

• *Obsession* (1976)

• *Taxi Driver* (1976)

• *The Yakuza* (1975)

My college writing teacher

was a funny bird. His class was extremely popular and wildly over-subscribed. He didn't show up the first day of class. Instead he left a note, "Write a five thousand word short story and put it under the door by six p.m. tomorrow or don't bother to come to another class." That eliminated eighty out of a hundred prospective students. At the next class, Dr. S. puffed a pipe and told us a story about his writing teacher, a man so senile that each week he repeated the previous week's anecdotes. Then Dr. S. read aloud the first few paragraphs of each of our stories doing his best to make them sound well written. Every week, he said, he would read our stories aloud. During the break ten more students disappeared. After the break Dr. S. again told us the story of the professor who was so senile that he kept telling the same stories over and over. As he proceeded to read our stories aloud again, three more dismayed students slipped out the back. For weeks Dr. S. began each class with the story of his senile teacher until finally someone couldn't stand it anymore and confronted him with the embarrassing fact that he was repeating himself. Dr. S. smiled. "At last," he said, "Someone is willing to risk telling the truth. It's the first requirement of any writer."

My first writing office was in Hollywood in the complex modestly named "The Crossroads of the World." Down the hall some people were developing a story in which world peace was achieved through mass meditation. Upstairs another group was developing a story in which a Christ-like leader miraculously ordained world peace. The two groups loathed each other. On the occasions when they met in the hall or courtyard, they would argue vociferously and threaten to sue each other. Neither movie got made and perhaps because of this, world peace was postponed. The upstairs group wrote a horror script then moved out.

In the office next door lived Bill, sixty, shaved head, tattooed, stocky, a writer of children's stories. On the door of his office were ten names, all female, to whom the postman was to deliver the mail and thus the checks. All the checks were really for Bill. He invented the pseudonyms because the children's publications for which he wrote favored stories by women authors and set limits on how many titles they would buy from the same writer in any given month. Bill let me read some of his work. He wrote adventure stories, full of heroics, with simple moral lessons that didn't come off as preachy.

Bill had started writing children's stories in prison where he was doing twenty years for armed robbery. Back when he was robbing banks, he told his neighbors he was a writer, made an audio tape of a typewriter typing, and put it on his apartment stereo whenever he went out to rob a bank. This "alibi" hadn't worked. At his trial, despite a neighbor's testimony that Bill was the hardest working writer imaginable, Bill could not produce even one page of writing to show for all his typing. (Had Bill been a real writer at that time, he would have known that this was perfectly normal.) In prison a vocation counselor suggested that Bill actually try writing, so Bill picked children's stories because that's what any prisoner looking for quick parole would choose. It turned out Bill had a knack for writing and started selling stories from prison. For a cut of the proceeds, the vocation counselor let Bill use his wife's name and mailing address to have the checks delivered. Unfortunately the parole board didn't cotton to Bill having a pseudonym, and it took him an extra five years to make parole. For the year or so that I knew Bill, the eighteen-hour-a-day typing was for real, and Bill managed to save enough money so that when his "husband" Frank got out of prison, Bill was able to surprise him with a lovely ranch house in Encino — all financed by Bill's children's stories.

So what does all this tell us about being a writer? Well for one thing, as my writing teacher said, you probably have to think of yourself as a courageous teller of truth; and like Bill, you also have to be a damn good liar and a con. No wonder it's so hard.

TOM SCHULMAN

Screenplays, written or co-written:

• *The Holy Man* (1998)

• *8 Heads in a Duffel Bag* (1997)

• *Medicine Man* (1992)

• *What About Bob?* (1991)

• *Dead Poets Society* (1989) *AA*

• *Honey, I Shrunk the Kids* (1989)

The

screenwriter, in many ways, is a mirror to life and the times in which he lives; the history of the screenwriter is also the history of history, as is all great storytelling. Radio writers are a disappearing breed, whose work was even more difficult, because their stories had to be made effective with the use of sound alone; television has inundated the entire world and may soon replace every medium with digital magic that will make every home a theater; you can already smell the global popcorn. But it depends, as did all the others, on the magic of the lonely writer, seated in a small room facing a blank piece of paper, challenged to create a life from the depths of this imagination, and knowing, in his tortured heart, that, except for moments like this, he will soon be forgotten.

But who won't?

MELVILLE SHAVELSON

Screenplays, written or co-written:

• *Yours, Mine and Ours (1968)*

• *Cast a Giant Shadow (1966)*

• *A New Kind of Love (1963)*

• *The Pigeon That Took Rome (1962)*

• *On the Double (1961)*

• *It Started in Naples (1960)*

• *The Five Pennies (1959)*

• *Houseboat (1958)*

• *Beau James (1957)*

• *The Seven Little Foys (1955)*

• *I'll See You in My Dreams (1951)*

• *Sorrowful Jones (1949)*

Television:

• *Ike: The War Years (1978)*

"You're a very talented writer,

but I don't think there's any way I can hire you."

Those words would have been disappointing coming from anyone. Coming from William Goldman, they were heart stopping. Castle Rock was developing an idea for a film called *Malice* and Goldman had been asked by the company to identify a young, new (read inexpensive) writer whom he could tutor on the screenplay.

I was twenty-seven and I'd never written a screenplay before, in fact I'd never *read* a screenplay before, but my first stageplay, *A Few Good Men*, was about to go into rehearsal for Broadway, and the script fell into the hands of a Castle Rock executive who passed it on to Goldman.

And the phone rang. My agent.

"Would you be interested in having lunch tomorrow afternoon with William Goldman to discuss a possible movie project?"

I told him that since Goldman was a remarkable novelist and screenwriter, two-time Academy Award winner, and my personal hero, that, yeah, I could probably squeeze him in.

I showed up at the designated restaurant on the upper East side. Goldman stood, extended his hand, and said it.

"You're a very talented writer, but I don't think there's any way I can hire you." Didn't look like I'd be getting lunch that day.

"I loved reading your play, but you've never written a screenplay, not even a lousy *television pilot*, and I don't think you have the experience necessary for us to be able to work on this." No lunch. No nothin'.

I told him that while I couldn't convince him that I had more experience than I did, perhaps I could convince him that experience wasn't crucial. I sat down. (The waiter eventually came and there was food.) We talked about the Mets and we talked about our mutual back problems, but mostly we talked about writing. Two hours later, my hero extended his hand again and said, "I tell you what: We've got a deal."

In the eight years and three films that followed, William Goldman taught me most of what I know about screenwriting, and a small fraction of what *he* knows. I'm very grateful.

Thanks for lunch, Bill. Really.

AARON SORKIN

Screenplays, written or co-written:

• *The American President* (1995)

• *Malice* (1993)

• *A Few Good Men* (1992)

"There's more...

there's more than just me. You can't break, my boy, even when there's nothing left...
now some people, we both know them, Al, think you can go stand in the middle of
the bullring and cry 'Mea Culpa, Mea Culpa,' while the crowd is hissing and booing
and spitting on you. But a man doesn't cry. I don't cry. You don't cry. You <u>fight!</u>"

— Richard Nixon to Alexander Haig in *Nixon*.
Written by Stephen J. Rivele, Christopher Wilkinson and Oliver Stone.

OLIVER STONE

Screenplays, written or co-written:

• *Evita* (1996)

• *Nixon* (1995)

• *Natural Born Killers* (1994)

• *Heaven and Earth* (1993)

• *JFK* (1991)

• *The Doors* (1991)

• *Born On the Fourth of July* (1989)

• *Talk Radio* (1988)

• *Wall Street* (1987)

• *Platoon* (1986)

• *Salvador* (1986)

• *Scarface* (1983)

• *Conan the Barbarian* (1982)

• *Midnight Express* (1978) *AA*

The writer is the architect of the film.

ROBIN SWICORD

Screenplays, written or co-written:

• Practical Magic (1998)

• Matilda (1996)

• The Perez Family (1995)

• Little Women (1994)

• Shag (1989)

Top Ten Cool Things
About Being A Screenwriter:

10. No heavy lifting

9. Get to grovel near director's chair

8. Polish actresses are hot for you

7. Carpal tunnel rarely fatal

6. Complimentary wash & lube on Maserati

5. No need to waste time looking for your name on lists of
   Hollywood's Most Powerful

4. Annual Easter egg hunt in Joe Eszterhas' beard

3. After "the big scene," high fives with Pauly Shore

2. Let's just say, they don't call it "Kinko's" for nothing

1. Shakespeare, shmakespeare!

TED TALLY

Screenplays, written or co-written:

• *Before and After* (1996)

• *The Juror* (1996)

• *The Silence of the Lambs* (1991) *AA*

• *White Palace* (1990)

Television:

• *The Father Clements Story* (1987)

                    KAREN

He was drunk when he came in... at five a.m. He looked
alarmed when he saw me. I was lying on the floor. Of
course, the baby was dead. It was a boy. But they worked
me over at the hospital and fixed me up fine. They even
took my appendix out. They threw that in for free.

                    WARDEN

Listen. Please. Listen.

                    KAREN

And, of course, one more thing -- no more children.
Do you know what that means? You're not a woman.
The meaning of it is gone. You're a gutted shell... Yes,
I went out with men after that -- and if I'd ever found
one that--

                    WARDEN

Listen! Listen to me --.

                    KAREN

All right. I'm listening.

Warden shakes his head, inarticulate with rage and love. He moves
closer to her.

                    KAREN

I know. Until I met you, I didn't think it was possible,
either.

                                        FADE OUT.

```
                    * * * * *

                   ALMA  (cont'd)
      ... and then I'll meet the proper man with the proper
      position. And I'll be a proper wife who can keep a
      proper home and raise proper children. And I will be
      happy because when you are proper you are safe.


      The victrola record ends. Alma turns away from Prew and goes
      to the victrola. Now that she's had her say with such cer-
      tainty, she deflates. Except for the fact that she looks like
      a girl who never cries, she looks as if she might cry.
      She lifts the record off the turntable.


                        ALMA
      But I do mean it when I say I need you. Because I'm
      lonely ...
                        (pause)
      You think I'm lying, don't you?


                        PREW
      No.  Nobody ever lies about being lonely...


      Alma puts the same record on again.


                     FADE  OUT.
```

— Karen Holmes and Milton Warden; Alma Lorene and Robert E. Lee Prewitt in *From Here to Eternity.*

DANIEL TARADASH

Screenplays:

• *Bell, Book and Candle* (1958)

• *Storm Center* (1956)

• *Picnic* (1955)

• *Desirée* (1954)

• *From Here to Eternity* (1953) *AA*

• *Don't Bother to Knock* (1952)

• *Rancho Notorious* (1952)

In 1942

the Warner Brothers theater in San Pedro and my father's place of business, the Towne Smart Shop, were both on 6th Street. While he sold dresses at $8.95 retail to the wives of merchant marines and tuna fishermen, I might find myself just across the street, comfortably ensconced in the daytime darkness of a movie matinee — both of us, it turned out, working at our respective professions, I all unwittingly.

My first memory of an actual movie was undoubtedly of a World War II film. A downed pilot lay on a small inflatable life raft floating on a very large ocean. The next thing I remember I was trying to walk into the screen until my mother, with some degree of justifiable panic, managed to pull me off the stage. This effort on my behalf — and the audience's for that matter — provided only a temporary measure of relief. One way or another I've been trying to work my way into that screen down to this day.

ROBERT TOWNE

Screenplays, written or co-written:

- *Without Limits (1998)*
- *Mission: Impossible (1996)*
- *Love Affair (1994)*
- *The Firm (1993)*
- *Days of Thunder (1990)*
- *The Two Jakes (1990)*
- *Tequila Sunrise (1988)*
- *Personal Best (1982)*
- *Shampoo (1975)*
- *The Yakuza (1975)*
- *Chinatown (1974) AA*
- *The Last Detail (1973)*
- *Villa Rides (1968)*
- *Tomb of Ligeia (1965)*
- *The Last Woman on Earth (1960)*

Movies are right up there with the Pen and the Sword and I love 'em.

MELVIN VAN PEEBLES

Screenplays:

• La Bonne a Tout Faire (1998)

• Panther (1995)

• Vroom Vroom Vroom (1994)

• Greased Lightning [co-written] (1977)

• Don't Play Us Cheap (1973)

• Sweet Sweetback's Baadasssss Song (1971)

• The Story of a Three-Day Pass (1968)

Television:

• Melvin Van Peebles' Classified "X" (1998)

The studios

are now copying successful pictures. They love number twos, number threes, number fours — because they already know what the "theme," as they would say it, is and it's just going to be a continuation of that thing.

If you bring them a story that is totally original, they say, "This is very interesting, but I've never seen it before." You say, " That is why I would like to make it!" "But how do we know it's going to be successful? Look, there are many nice things here, but I'm not familiar with them. I would have sleepless nights because this will be a thirty-million-dollar picture, and it's never been tried before."

It was not that tough back then as it is today, because I don't think I ever made a picture that cost more than two or three million dollars. But they made fifty pictures then. Now it becomes that enormous something . . . and people who have not grown up in the motion picture industry are looking over your shoulder as the script is being written and say, "My God, we're gonna be dead, we're gonna dismiss secretaries, policemen, Credit Lyonnais is going to cut off our credit . . ." You used to make good pictures, very good pictures, lousy pictures, but if you made five big hits that year, you were even and you went on. It was not like you were shooting the New Testament, that this would be the beginning and the end of everything. Just a picture.

— From the Writers Guild Foundation series *The Writer Speaks,* 1995

BILLY WILDER

Screenplays co-written:

- *Avanti! (1972)*
- *The Fortune Cookie (1966)*
- *The Apartment (1960) AA*
- *Some Like it Hot (1959)*
- *Witness for the Prosecution (1957)*
- *The Seven Year Itch (1955)*
- *Sabrina (1954)*
- *Stalag 17 (1953)*
- *The Big Carnival (1951)*
- *Sunset Boulevard (1950) AA*
- *A Foreign Affair (1948)*
- *The Lost Weekend (1945) AA*
- *Double Indemnity (1944)*
- *Ball of Fire (1941)*
- *Hold Back the Dawn (1941)*
- *Ninotchka (1939)*

I remember

my father scarring our dining room table with razor blades.

He was cutting sometimes-long pieces of quarter-inch-wide recording tape on it (without newspaper underneath, which my mother begged him to use), splicing them together with little pieces of Scotch tape, twirling them back onto an even-then old reel-to-reel recorder, and playing them back, over and over, as he made — as he built — piece by piece — a radio documentary called *Here in These Fields*.

I remember seeing this — hearing it: the recorded voices of his subjects and his own wafting through the house (he never used earphones, though he certainly could have). But I also remember thinking nothing of it; it was just what he did for a time; it was his job for a time. That was all.

One never seems to realize (except in movies) the moments — as they're happening — that will influence one most significantly. My father working on his radio documentaries in our dining room is one of them. Looking back on my own work, which I try to do as infrequently as possible, bring this "forgotten memory," this influence, back. Of course there are others, all part of a pattern I see now, part of a foundation, perhaps even more than that, for everything I do.

STEVEN ZAILLIAN

Screenplays:

• *A Civil Action* (1998)

• *Clear and Present Danger* [co-written] (1994)

• *Schindler's List* (1993) *AA*

• *Searching for Bobby Fischer* (1993)

• *Jack the Bear* (1993)

• *Awakenings* (1990)

• *The Falcon and the Snowman* (1985)

The life

of everyone on board depends on just one thing: finding somebody back there who not only can fly this plane, but who didn't have fish for dinner!

— Dr. Rumack in *Airplane!*

DAVID ZUCKER

Screenplays co-written:

• *The Naked Gun 33 1/3: The Final Insult!* (1994)

• *Naked Gun 2 1/2: The Smell of Fear!* (1991)

• *The Naked Gun:*

   From the Files of Police Squad! (1989)

• *Top Secret!* (1984)

• *Airplane!* (1980)

• *The Kentucky Fried Movie* (1977)

JIM ABRAHAMS

Screenplays co-written:

• *Jane Austen's Mafia!* (1998)

• *Hot Shots! Part Deux* (1993)

• *The Naked Gun:*

   From the Files of Police Squad! (1989)

• *Hot Shots!* (1991)

• *Top Secret!* (1984)

• *Airplane!* (1980)

• *The Kentucky Fried Movie* (1977)

JERRY ZUCKER

Screenplays co-written:

• *The Naked Gun:*

   From the Files of Police Squad! (1989)

• *Top Secret!* (1984)

• *Airplane!* (1980)

• *The Kentucky Fried Movie* (1977)

Index

Thank you.

For noticing and supporting the idea when it was only that: Jamie Smith, Debbie Thurman, Scott Roeben and Pat Duncan.

For invaluable support with this project and beyond: Writers Guild of America, especially the Board of Directors, the Writers' Image Campaign Committee, Property Art Committee, Cheryl Rhoden, Scott Roeben, Sean Costello and Del Reisman.

For superior craftsmanship in lab work and printing: Paris Photo Lab, Los Angeles.

For materializing a vision and making us proud of the excellence of the Finnish graphic industry: Erweko Printing House, Metsä Serla Art Paper Mill and Lito-Scan, Finland.

For turning every element into a true tribute to craftsmanship: graphic designer Ilkka Kärkkäinen.

For taking the portraits collection on a European tour: Moving Pictures (Cannes exhibit); Ulrike Hager, Viola Winokan, Studio Babelsberg and TNT (Berlin exhibit); Martti Lundström, Pauliina Valpas, AVEK and DHL Helsinki (Helsinki exhibit and workshop).

For unparalleled professionalism: Ellen Harrington, Robert Smolkin and Leslie Unger at the Academy of Motion Picture Arts and Sciences, Beverly Hills.

For admirable persistence: our literary agent Priscilla Palmer.

For understanding that all the above shouldn't be wasted: Paddy Calistro and Scott McAuley of Angel City Press.

About the authors

"Writers are a primary creative force behind a movie, but practically invisible to the moviegoers of the world. I hope that — at least while viewing these portraits — readers will look at movies in terms of the writers' creative role."

In her first award-winning book, *The Creative Manifesto*, Helena Lumme photographed top European talents as beggars on the streets and social outcasts. "When mediocracy rules, excellence becomes a beggar."

Helena Lumme, BA, author and communication strategist who resides in Los Angeles, enjoys tackling issues of perception that for some might seem impossible to change. One such issue is the denigration of the screenwriter, which has continued for decades. Helena's studies in creativity have led her to understand the complexity of recognition.

"Creative people don't thrive on power and visibility — their priority is to create. That is one reason why Hollywood has had it so easy keeping writers in the background. But in doing so it has also created deep injustice, and given us incomplete information about the real author of the movie."

There is no doubt in Helena's mind that the success of the American film industry is built upon the superior craft of screenwriters. "They have the ability to tell universally touching stories, which is the most difficult part of moviemaking."

Helena created the idea of a portrait collection and a book that would make the writers' contributions better known. She and photographer Mika Manninen built a collection of visual and verbal portraits of some of the world's most prominent screenwriters today. Helena approached private sponsors and foundations in order to exhibit the portraits in Cannes at the Cannes Film Festival, Berlin at the European Film Awards, Helsinki at the Taidehalli art museum, and Los Angeles at the Academy of Motion Picture Arts and Sciences, and to compile the portraits into this book.

"This tribute to American screenwriters is long overdue," says Helena, who through her company Sincere Image also creates new types of communication strategies for high-profile corporations and organizations.

Helena Lumme

"Writers have a captivating charisma. Their faces are full of stories, told and untold. I admire their courage to be themselves, and to open up their souls for every piece of work they do — their movies as well as these portraits."

Mika Manninen is known for his skillful, warm and humorous portraits of musicians, filmmakers and artists. His photographic work has appeared in *Vanity Fair, Fast Company,* and graced the covers of many books and compact discs in Europe and the United States. Mika also shoots lifestyle advertising for international brands such as Coca-Cola, Levi's, and Sony. He works as comfortably with moving images, shooting commercials and short films.

Whether building exhibitions or making films, Mika and Helena work together as a film team: Helena writes and directs, Mika shoots. Photographing America's storytellers took the couple nine months.

"We wanted to photograph each writer in a place where he or she felt the most comfortable. Most of the writers chose their homes," Mika explains. "The shooting itself was fast and simple, while laying the groundwork, scheduling, and raising money to be able to go on consumed most of our time. This project was my university in filmmaking," confesses Mika.

This book allows Helena and Mika to share their personal journey with the reader. They hope to see screenwriters gain a more visible part in American film history. "Studios, publicists or photo editors used to think screenwriters weren't worth photographing. Many brilliant screenwriters have passed away without future generations ever having a decent photo of them," concludes Mika.

The original prints of this portrait collection are part of Writers Guild of America's permanent collection.

Mika Manninen

Fade ou